THE VITALIST SEES THE SIGNS

GB Clarkson is a poet of Irish heritage whose work has been anthologised in *This Line is Not for Turning: An Anthology of Contemporary British Prose Poetry*, ed. Jane Monson (Cinnamon Press, 2011), *Furies: a Poetry Anthology of Women Warriors*, ed. Eve Lacey (For Books' Sake, 2014), *The Valley Press Anthology of Prose Poetry*, ed. Anne Caldwell (Valley Press, 2019) and *Witches, Warriors, Workers: an anthology of contemporary working women's poetry*, ed. Fran Lock & Jane Burn (Culture Matters, 2020).

Also by GB Clarkson

Singletary   (Shearsman Books, 2025)

Medlars   (Shearsman Books, 2023)

Crucifox   (Verve Poetry Press, 2021)

Monica's Overcoat of Flesh   (Nine Arches Press, 2020)

No. 25   (Shearsman Books, 2018)

Dora Incites the Sea-Scribbler to Lament   (Smith | Doorstop, 2016)

Declare   (Shearsman Books, 2016)

CONTENTS

ISBN: 978-1-917617-40-6

Cover designed by Aaron Kent

Edited and Typeset by Aaron Kent

Broken Sleep Books Ltd
PO BOX 102
Llandysul
SA44 9BG

The Vitalist Sees the Signs

GB Clarkson

Broken Sleep Books

THE VITALIST CREAMS OFF THE PROPHETS

The Vitalist is not crude, and has a full head of sublimations. From Amos to Zechariah, she knows her stuff. She eyes up Isaiah, handles Hosea, and has an octobrach broken tongue which crumbles like butterbread if she comes out with truth and wise saws. Biting back deeper matter, the Vitalist is sore.

THE VITALIST FINDS EMPLOYMENT IN A FUNERAL PARLOUR,

where, in a back room, she helps devise new merchandise: 'Ashes to Casserole Dishes', 'Departed Fistbumps', 'Relax Relics & Grief Salts for the Bath'—and other dead-friendly ventures. She fantasises about a 'Lock-it Locket' wearable key—which secures a door you never want to open again. Her bosses are impressed and though she works for a sub-living wage, without holiday or sick pay, there are posthumous perks, and a coffin thrown in. Also use of the garage as a gym when it is empty.

Treadmill of the dead.

THE VITALIST ENDURES A WINTER'S TALE

Lost, she then loses everything she has, as a kind of revenge. She loses her parents, her siblings, her children, co-workers, home, country, dentist. She is cold and angry and the wind burns her naked and icy, but quite dry, and she bokes a winterword.

THE VITALIST ESCAPES PURGATORY

There, that wasn't that hard, was it.

THE VITALIST RE-READS PAGE 263,

and, this time, cries.

THE VITALIST GOES VILE

Vile vile to market

and buys spider crabs

Vile vile home again

to scald them and scold

her children for shunning

the webby flesh and scold

the crabs for refusing to pay

attention to a deep green book

with seascaped frontispiece

THE VITALIST HAS INSOMNIA

The Vitalist's heart whines in the small cells, red training to be blue. In a safety tangle, the king is impatient for his ship, a cement pull to the seabed. Time is a would-be pirate sharpening daggers in the desert. The Vitalist thinks herself into a Joshua tree.

with delicate jelly-like segments arching to a barb. She imagines eating them on sterile platters, slicing them lengthways, getting a little excited with each sting and transmuting it to blessing.

THE VITALIST HAS 10 DAYS TO GO,

slaughters a lamb, scours the pine tables, buys lemon-coloured curtains and flowers, grinds coffee and pepper, makes lists, reconnects with a penpal in Canada, compares life stories, compassionates others' lacks, apologises, takes a penknife to the stucco walls to make her mark, rubbing ochre into the newly stabbed pocks, a rustic charm. On the seventh day she opens all the curtains and windows and lets in gales of fierce July. She sweeps the floor of all shavings and wall-fallings. Outs spiders and silverfish. Her mind is a backyard with tin baths clanking across on a Saturday afternoon. On the eighth day she begins cooking, elaborating a sharp marinade and thumbing through terracotta basins for herbs.

THE VITALIST AND GEORGE ELIOT GO ON HOLIDAY TOGETHER

They wear lace caps. They chatter under the towering funnels and masts of the passenger steamships in the port jutting up into the low clouds of the grey day. George Eliot wants to circle the earth in search of successive autumns like a bird. The Vitalist envisages spring in Vienna. They tussle, mildly. Later George Eliot declares, heaving her black portmanteau onto a bunk bed in the cabin, that the highest—*most moral*—thing of all is *sweet abnegation, delicious self-denial*—and so they must live on holiday as if they'd never migrated. The Vitalist is beguiled by this idea of *non-life*, advocated with such clarity and enthusiasm, as well as by the nothingy pale sea which has started putting on a performance for the new passengers through the steamy porthole. She bags the top bunk. For the next 14 days, including 3 given over to mal de mer, she observes George Eliot rising shortly after 4am, rebuttoning her floor-length nightdress, exchanging a linen night cap for the winged-lace day cap and laying out a bank of gold-nibbed pens and sepia pages by the candlestick on the cabin desk. GE's face is all hollows and angles as she focuses. Her eyes lift occasionally to the cabin walls and she seems to scan fully peopled cities in the whorls of the honey-coloured timbers, then untold vistas in the undulations and desultory white horses of the dingy sea, always rearing up and climbing the eternal O of the porthole. The Vitalist meditates on the top bunk, sharpens pencils, chops candies and nuts, letting them down in a crocheted pouch to the lower bunk, along with occasional notes offering to do GE's laundry and making random observations. They breakfast on pastries some goodly period past their best, and raisins and half-oranges. After a fortnight they call at a port which the Vitalist does not catch the name of. GE has booked ahead at a pension run by three rosy landlady-philosophers, who take it in turns to speak, a third of a sentence each, bestowing verbs, nouns and particles equally and equably between their interlocutors. *Suffering ennobles the crudest creatures*, George proclaims, fretting for a pen. The Vitalist supplies a jotter, opened at a page hurriedly titled 'Tribulations'. They accept an attic room which looks out over red roofs and a crooked blue sky. The leaves on the trees show a definite twist of autumn. The Vitalist dreams of cherry blossom.

THE VITALIST SPENDS TIME WITH JOHN DONNE

He has her try out a coffin but it's too short for her to lie in. She sits, legs bent up near her belly and he places two silk cushions, one, salmon pink, at the small of her back, and the other, crimson, below her knees. Then parades peacocks past her window, vaunting themselves against the rose-trellises which are decorated with Celtic knotwork—he knows her proclivities. 'Batter my heart!' she exclaims. He fiddles with his nails and an ax.

THE VITALIST GATHERS UP IMAGES TO SOOTHE HER MIND

Cobalt butterflies and ivory blossom in close-up, Dalí paintings, peacocks, curlicued bookcovers from the nineteenth century, one and a half lines from Coleridge. Her mind puffs out, diseased, but resisting.

THE VITALIST MEETS KATHERINE MANSFIELD AND
THEY PREPARE GREAT PARTY FOOD TOGETHER

Baked eggs, poached apricots with ginger, cheese straws; anchovies. Black coffee. Mirabelle. Whiskey. De-crusted sandwiches layered with lemon curd, marmalade & handsome gooseberry jam. Elderflower jelly. Brown-speckled fish flounces. Whipped cream puffs, stacked shakily high. Orange soufflé. Coldwater scones with plentiful butter. A basket of berries. Tiny blue saucers of redcurrant jelly. Whole celestial cheeses. Limes. Gold plums. Hare soup. Stuffing balls. Platters of ham. Masses of mustardy rolls, spruced with spider crab.

THE VITALIST WADES THROUGH A BOG OF MISOGYNY

a stinkhorned off-white mess like sour cream, hiding stinging fish and sink holes, a whole sucking morass between her and the next milestone, a whole smirking mire.

THE VITALIST VISITS THE DEAD ZONES OF THE SEA

Having been given an index, she set out to log each one. She's a mourner-tourist, three-hanky mariner, with no skill to reverse, only to observe and record, and wail internally. She tries psychic healing. Children murmur, mermaids cheer.

ACKNOWLEDGEMENTS

Thank you to Aaron Kent and the Broken Sleep team for selecting this sequence, and for the sensitive editorial suggestions. Also thanks to Kelvin Corcoran and Tony Frazer who previously published some of these pieces in *Shearsman Magazine*.

LAY OUT YOUR UNREST

www.ingramcontent.com/pod-product-compliance
Lightning Source LLC
LaVergne TN
LVHW041239080426
835508LV00011B/1284